Disclaimer

The author and publisher do not accept any liability for any misapplication or problems that may arise from following the advice or using the information contained in this book. It is the reader's responsibility to use their own judgment and consult with appropriate professionals before making any business decisions. The publisher and the author assume no liability for any errors or omissions or for any actions taken based on the information contained in this book.

First printing, 2023.
SKU Ref: HRG014

Cover image created with Dall-E.

HRreview
Black and White Trading Ltd
23 Templemere
Weybridge
Surrey
United Kingdom
KT13 9PA

www.hrreview.co.uk

# Contents

# Introduction

Neurodiversity refers to the natural variation in human brain function and the different ways in which people process information. Neurodivergent conditions, such as autism, ADHD, and dyslexia, affect a significant portion of the population, and many of these individuals can face challenges in the workplace.

However, accommodating neurodiversity in the workplace can have significant benefits for businesses. By creating a supportive and inclusive work environment, businesses can increase productivity, improve employee engagement, and foster innovation.

In this white paper, we will explore the concept of neurodiversity and its relevance to the workplace. We will provide an overview of common neurodivergent conditions and the accommodations that can help support neurodiverse employees. We will also discuss the legal considerations involved in accommodating neurodiversity and provide guidance on how businesses can create an inclusive workplace culture.

Finally, we will examine the business case for neurodiversity, exploring the ROI for businesses that prioritize accommodations for neurodiverse employees. By the end of this white paper, readers will have a comprehensive understanding of neurodiversity in the workplace and the benefits of accommodating neurodiversity.

# Section 1 – Defining Neurodiversity

# What is Neurodiversity?

Neurodiversity refers to the natural variation in human brain function and the different ways in which people process information. It recognizes that there is no "normal" or "standard" brain, and that there are many different ways of thinking and processing information that are equally valid.

The term "neurodiversity" was first coined in the late 1990s by Australian sociologist Judy Singer, who sought to shift the focus away from the negative aspects of neurological differences and toward a more positive and inclusive approach.

Neurodivergent conditions are those that affect the way individuals process information, learn, and interact with others. These conditions can include autism, ADHD, dyslexia, dyscalculia, Tourette's syndrome, and others. While individuals with these conditions may experience challenges in certain areas, they can also have unique strengths and abilities that can benefit the workplace.

It's important to recognize and embrace neurodiversity in the workplace because it can lead to increased innovation, creativity, and problem-solving. Additionally, accommodating the needs of neurodiverse employees can improve employee engagement and productivity.

In the next section, we will explore the various neurodivergent conditions that can affect employees and discuss the challenges they may face in the workplace.

# What are the Main Neurodivergent Conditions?

Neurodivergent conditions are those that affect the way individuals process information, learn, and interact with others. These conditions can include autism, ADHD, dyslexia, dyscalculia, Tourette's syndrome, and others.

Individuals with autism may experience challenges with social interactions, communication, and sensory processing. They may have difficulty understanding nonverbal cues or expressing their own emotions, and may be sensitive to certain sounds, lights, or textures.

- **ADHD** can affect an individual's ability to focus, prioritize tasks, and manage time. Individuals with ADHD may struggle with organization, impulsivity, and hyperactivity.
- **Dyslexia** is a learning disorder that affects reading and language processing. Individuals with dyslexia may have difficulty with phonological processing, recognizing written words, and understanding the meaning of sentences.
- **Dyscalculia** is a condition that affects an individual's ability to understand and work with numbers. Individuals with dyscalculia may have difficulty with basic arithmetic, understanding mathematical concepts, and using numbers in real-world situations.
- **Tourette's syndrome** is a neurological condition characterized by repetitive, involuntary movements and vocalizations called tics. These tics can be disruptive and may affect an individual's social interactions and self-esteem.

Individuals with neurodivergent conditions may experience challenges in the workplace, including difficulty with social interactions, communication, and executive functioning.

However, they can also have unique strengths and abilities that can benefit the workplace. For example, individuals with autism may have exceptional attention to detail and analytical skills, while individuals with ADHD may be highly creative and innovative.

# How is Neurodiversity Different from Mental Illness?

Neurodiversity is different from mental illness in that it refers to natural variations in human brain function and the different ways in which people process information. It recognizes that there is no "normal" or "standard" brain, and that there are many different ways of thinking and processing information that are equally valid. Neurodivergent conditions, such as autism, ADHD, and dyslexia, are examples of variations in brain function that can affect the way individuals process information, learn, and interact with others.

On the other hand, mental illness refers to a broad range of conditions that affect an individual's mood, behavior, and thinking patterns. These conditions can include depression, anxiety, bipolar disorder, schizophrenia, and others. While some individuals with neurodivergent conditions may also experience symptoms of mental illness, the two concepts are not the same.

It's important to distinguish between neurodivergent conditions and mental illness because doing so helps to avoid stigmatizing or pathologizing natural variations in human brain function. Additionally, understanding the differences between neurodiversity and mental illness can help employers and co-workers to provide appropriate support and accommodations for individuals with different needs.

# Why is Neurodiversity Important in the Workplace?

Accommodating neurodiversity in the workplace is important because it can lead to significant benefits for both individuals and businesses. Research has shown that neurodiverse employees can bring valuable skills and perspectives to the workplace, including increased innovation, creativity, and problem-solving skills.

Neurodivergent individuals often have unique ways of processing information, which can lead to fresh insights and ideas that may not be apparent to neurotypical individuals. They may also be highly detail-oriented and skilled at pattern recognition, which can be beneficial in industries such as technology, engineering, and finance.

Moreover, by creating an inclusive and accommodating workplace culture, businesses can improve employee engagement and retention. When employees feel valued and supported, they are more likely to be productive, motivated, and loyal to their employer.

There is also a growing demand among consumers for businesses that prioritize diversity and inclusion. By accommodating neurodiversity in the workplace, businesses can demonstrate their commitment to social responsibility and attract a wider customer base.

In addition to these benefits, businesses that accommodate neurodiverse employees may also be more likely to comply with legal requirements and regulations, such as the Americans with Disabilities Act (ADA) and other relevant laws.

Overall, accommodating neurodiversity in the workplace can lead to a more diverse, productive, and innovative workforce. In the next section, we will explore the different accommodations and support that can be provided to neurodiverse employees in the workplace.

# Section 2 - Accommodating Neurodiverse Employees

# Common Accommodations for Neurodiverse Employees

To support neurodiverse employees in the workplace, it's important to provide accommodations that address their specific needs. Some common accommodations that can help neurodiverse employees thrive in the workplace include:

1. **Flexible work arrangements:** Providing flexible work arrangements, such as the ability to work from home or adjust work hours, can be beneficial for neurodiverse employees who may need a quieter or more comfortable environment to work effectively.
2. **Sensory-friendly environments:** Reducing noise levels, providing visual aids, and ensuring adequate lighting can create a sensory-friendly environment that can help neurodiverse employees feel more comfortable and focused.
3. **Assistive technology:** Assistive technology, such as speech-to-text software, noise-cancelling headphones, and ergonomic keyboards, can help neurodiverse employees work more efficiently and effectively.
4. **Specialized training and support:** Providing specialized training and support, such as coaching, mentoring, and counseling, can help neurodiverse employees develop their skills and navigate the workplace more successfully.

It's important to note that accommodations will vary depending on the specific needs of each individual employee. It's also important to involve neurodiverse employees in the accommodation process and to provide ongoing support and feedback to ensure that accommodations are effective.

Providing these accommodations can not only support neurodiverse employees, but can also benefit the business by improving productivity, reducing turnover, and creating a more inclusive workplace culture. In the next section, we will discuss the legal considerations surrounding accommodations for neurodiverse employees.

## Legal Considerations

**In the UK,** businesses have a legal obligation to provide reasonable accommodations for employees with disabilities under the Equality Act 2010. This includes neurodiverse employees who may require accommodations to perform their job duties effectively.

Under the Equality Act, an individual is considered disabled if they have a physical or mental impairment that has a substantial and long-term adverse effect on their ability to carry out normal day-to-day activities. This can include individuals with neurodivergent conditions such as autism, ADHD, and dyslexia.

To comply with the Equality Act, businesses must take reasonable steps to ensure that employees with disabilities can perform their job duties effectively. This may include providing accommodations such as assistive technology, flexible work arrangements, and specialized training and support.

It's important for businesses to be aware of the legal requirements surrounding accommodations for neurodiverse employees and to take proactive steps to ensure compliance. This may include developing policies and procedures for requesting accommodations, training managers and supervisors on how to provide accommodations, and creating a culture that is supportive of neurodiversity.

In addition to legal obligations, accommodating neurodiverse employees can also lead to business benefits such as increased productivity, engagement, and innovation. By creating an inclusive workplace culture that supports neurodiversity, businesses can attract and retain a diverse range of talented employees.

**In the US,** businesses have a legal obligation to provide reasonable accommodations for employees with disabilities under the Americans with Disabilities Act (ADA). This includes neurodiverse employees who may require accommodations to perform their job duties effectively.

Under the ADA, an individual is considered disabled if they have a physical or mental impairment that substantially limits one or more major life activities, such as learning or communicating. This can include individuals with neurodivergent conditions such as autism, ADHD, and dyslexia.

To comply with the ADA, businesses must take reasonable steps to ensure that employees with disabilities can perform their job duties effectively. This may include providing accommodations such as assistive technology, flexible work arrangements, and specialized training and support.

It's important for businesses to be aware of the legal requirements surrounding accommodations for neurodiverse employees and to take proactive steps to ensure compliance. This may include developing policies and procedures for requesting accommodations, training managers and supervisors on how to provide accommodations, and creating a culture that is supportive of neurodiversity.

In addition to legal obligations, accommodating neurodiverse employees can also lead to business benefits such as increased productivity, engagement, and innovation. By creating an inclusive workplace culture that supports neurodiversity, businesses can attract and retain a diverse range of talented employees.

It's important to note that state and local laws may also provide additional protections for individuals with disabilities. Therefore, businesses should consult with legal counsel to ensure that they are in compliance with all relevant laws and regulations.

# Creating an Inclusive Workplace Culture

To support neurodiverse employees in the workplace, it's important to create an inclusive workplace culture that values diversity and promotes understanding and acceptance of neurodivergent conditions.

Some strategies for creating an inclusive workplace culture include:

1. **Providing education and awareness:** Educating employees on the concept of neurodiversity, its benefits, and the specific needs of neurodivergent individuals can help to reduce stigma and increase understanding.
2. **Encouraging open communication:** Encouraging open communication between neurodiverse employees and their co-workers and managers can help to ensure that their needs are being met and that they are comfortable and supported in the workplace.
3. **Providing support and resources:** Providing support and resources, such as coaching, mentoring, and counseling, can help neurodiverse employees navigate the workplace and develop their skills and strengths.
4. **Fostering a culture of acceptance:** Fostering a culture of acceptance and celebrating the unique strengths and abilities of neurodiverse employees can help to create a positive and inclusive workplace environment.
5. **Making accommodations visible:** Making accommodations visible and normalizing their use can help to reduce the stigma associated with requesting accommodations and encourage more employees to take advantage of them.

By creating an inclusive workplace culture that supports neurodiversity, businesses can not only attract and retain a diverse range of talented employees but also promote innovation, productivity, and engagement.

In conclusion, accommodating neurodiversity in the workplace is not only a legal and ethical responsibility but also a smart business decision. By providing accommodations and creating an inclusive workplace culture, businesses can unlock the full potential of their neurodiverse employees and reap the benefits of a diverse and innovative workforce.

## Some Real-World Examples

Many businesses have already recognized the benefits of accommodating neurodiverse employees and have implemented successful strategies to support them in the workplace. Here are some real-world examples:

Microsoft: Microsoft has a dedicated program, the Autism Hiring Program, that focuses on hiring individuals with autism for full-time positions. The program provides specialized training, support, and accommodations to help these employees succeed in the workplace.

- **SAP:** SAP has a program called Autism at Work, which focuses on hiring individuals with autism for full-time positions in a variety of roles. The program provides specialized training and support, as well as accommodations such as flexible work arrangements and sensory-friendly workspaces.
- **EY:** EY has launched a neurodiversity program called EY Neurodiversity Inclusion Center of Excellence (NICE), which focuses on hiring and supporting neurodiverse employees. The program provides specialized training, support, and accommodations, as well as a network of mentors and peers for neurodiverse employees.
- **JP Morgan:** JP Morgan has launched a program called Autism at Work, which focuses on hiring individuals with autism for full-time positions in technology and other areas. The program provides specialized training and support, as well as accommodations such as flexible work arrangements and sensory-friendly workspaces.

These are just a few examples of businesses that have successfully implemented strategies to support neurodiverse employees. By providing accommodations, specialized training, and support, these businesses have been able to unlock the full potential of their neurodiverse employees and create a more diverse and innovative workforce.

In conclusion, businesses that prioritize and accommodate neurodiversity in the workplace can benefit from increased innovation, productivity, and employee engagement. By implementing strategies such as flexible work arrangements, sensory-friendly environments, and specialized training and support, businesses can create an inclusive workplace culture that values diversity and promotes the success of all employees.

# Section 4 - Common Accommodations for Neurodiverse Employees

# Understanding the Needs of Neurodiverse Employees

To provide effective accommodations for neurodiverse employees, it's important to understand their specific needs and potential barriers they may face in the workplace.

Neurodiverse employees may have different ways of processing information and interacting with others, which can impact their work performance. For example, employees with autism may struggle with social interactions and sensory sensitivities, while employees with ADHD may have difficulty with executive functioning and staying organized.

By understanding the needs of neurodiverse employees, businesses can provide accommodations that support their success in the workplace. This may include accommodations such as assistive technology, flexible work arrangements, and specialized training and support.

It's important to involve neurodiverse employees in the accommodation process to ensure that accommodations are effective and meet their specific needs. This can include conducting regular check-ins and feedback sessions, providing coaching and mentoring, and creating opportunities for open communication and collaboration.

Additionally, businesses can provide training and resources for managers and co-workers to better understand the needs of neurodiverse employees and create a supportive and inclusive workplace culture. By promoting understanding and acceptance of neurodiversity, businesses can create a more diverse and innovative workforce.

In conclusion, understanding the needs of neurodiverse employees is key to providing effective accommodations and creating an inclusive workplace culture. By taking a proactive approach to supporting neurodiversity, businesses can benefit from increased productivity, engagement, and innovation from all employees.

# Accommodations for Communication Needs

Effective communication is essential in any workplace, but it can be particularly challenging for neurodiverse employees who may struggle with verbal and written communication. To support these employees, businesses can provide accommodations such as:

1. **Assistive technology:** Assistive technology such as speech-to-text software, text-to-speech software, and alternative keyboards can help neurodiverse employees communicate more effectively in the workplace.
2. **Visual aids:** Visual aids such as diagrams, flowcharts, and infographics can help neurodiverse employees understand complex information more easily and communicate their ideas more clearly.
3. **Alternative communication methods:** For employees who struggle with verbal communication, alternative communication methods such as email, chat, and instant messaging can be helpful. These methods can provide a way for employees to communicate without the added pressure of face-to-face interactions.
4. **Clear and direct communication:** Providing clear and direct communication, with specific instructions and expectations, can help neurodiverse employees understand their roles and responsibilities and reduce confusion and anxiety.

It's important to involve neurodiverse employees in the accommodation process to ensure that accommodations are effective and meet their specific needs. Providing these accommodations can not only support neurodiverse employees but can also benefit the business by improving communication and collaboration among all employees.

In addition to these accommodations, businesses can also foster a workplace culture that values clear communication and provides opportunities for all employees to share their ideas and perspectives. By creating a culture that supports and values neurodiversity, businesses can promote a more inclusive and innovative workplace environment.

## Accommodations for Sensory Needs

Many neurodiverse employees may have sensory sensitivities that can impact their work performance. These sensitivities may include sensitivity to noise, light, temperature, and texture.

To support neurodiverse employees with sensory needs, businesses can provide accommodations such as:

- **Noise-cancelling headphones:** Providing noise-cancelling headphones or earplugs can help neurodiverse employees block out distracting or overwhelming noise and focus on their work tasks.
- **Sensory-friendly workspaces:** Creating a sensory-friendly workspace that minimizes bright lights, loud noises, and other sensory distractions can help neurodiverse employees feel more comfortable and reduce stress.
- **Adjustments to lighting and temperature:** Adjusting lighting and temperature levels to meet the needs of neurodiverse employees can help create a more comfortable and productive work environment.
- **Flexible work arrangements:** Providing flexible work arrangements such as telecommuting or flexible hours can give neurodiverse employees more control over their work environment and reduce sensory overload.

It's important to involve neurodiverse employees in the accommodation process to ensure that accommodations are effective and meet their specific needs. Businesses can also provide education and resources for managers and co-workers to better understand the needs of neurodiverse employees and create a supportive and inclusive workplace culture.

By providing accommodations for sensory needs, businesses can create a more comfortable and productive work environment for all employees. This can lead to increased productivity, engagement, and innovation, and a more inclusive workplace culture that values diversity and promotes success for all employees.

In conclusion, accommodating the sensory needs of neurodiverse employees is essential for creating a supportive and inclusive workplace culture. By providing accommodations such as noise-cancelling headphones, sensory-friendly workspaces, and adjustments to lighting and temperature, businesses can create a more comfortable and productive work environment for all employees.

# Accommodations for Executive Functioning Needs

Executive functioning refers to a set of cognitive processes that allow individuals to plan, organize, and complete tasks. Many neurodiverse employees may struggle with executive functioning, which can impact their work performance.

To support neurodiverse employees with executive functioning needs, businesses can provide accommodations such as:

1. **Structured work tasks:** Providing clear and structured work tasks with specific deadlines and expectations can help neurodiverse employees stay organized and on-task.
2. **Visual schedules:** Providing visual schedules or checklists can help neurodiverse employees understand the sequence of tasks and prioritize their work.
3. **Prioritization tools:** Providing tools for prioritizing tasks, such as time management apps or project management software, can help neurodiverse employees manage their workload and stay on track.
4. **Coaching and mentoring:** Providing coaching and mentoring can help neurodiverse employees develop their executive functioning skills and learn strategies for managing their workload.

It's important to involve neurodiverse employees in the accommodation process to ensure that accommodations are effective and meet their specific needs. Businesses can also provide education and resources for managers and co-workers to better understand the needs of neurodiverse employees and create a supportive and inclusive workplace culture.

By providing accommodations for executive functioning needs, businesses can help neurodiverse employees stay organized and productive in the workplace. This can lead to increased productivity, engagement, and innovation, and a more inclusive workplace culture that values diversity and promotes success for all employees.

In conclusion, accommodating the executive functioning needs of neurodiverse employees is essential for creating a supportive and inclusive workplace culture. By providing structured work tasks, visual schedules, prioritization tools, and coaching and mentoring, businesses can support neurodiverse employees and unlock their full potential in the workplace.

# Accommodations for Social Interaction Needs

Many neurodiverse employees may struggle with social interactions, which can impact their work performance. To support these employees, businesses can provide accommodations such as:

1. **Coaching and mentoring:** Providing coaching and mentoring can help neurodiverse employees develop their social skills and learn strategies for interacting with co-workers and clients.
2. **Team-building activities:** Providing team-building activities that are designed to build social connections and promote collaboration can help neurodiverse employees feel more comfortable in social situations.
3. **Sensory-friendly social events:** Hosting sensory-friendly social events, such as low-key gatherings with quieter environments and reduced sensory input, can help neurodiverse employees feel more comfortable in social situations.
4. **Clear communication:** Providing clear and direct communication, with specific instructions and expectations, can help neurodiverse employees understand their roles and responsibilities and reduce confusion and anxiety.

It's important to involve neurodiverse employees in the accommodation process to ensure that accommodations are effective and meet their specific needs. Businesses can also provide education and resources for managers and co-workers to better understand the needs of neurodiverse employees and create a supportive and inclusive workplace culture.

By providing accommodations for social interaction needs, businesses can help neurodiverse employees feel more comfortable and supported in the workplace. This can lead to increased productivity, engagement, and innovation, and a more inclusive workplace culture that values diversity and promotes success for all employees.

In conclusion, accommodating the social interaction needs of neurodiverse employees is essential for creating a supportive and inclusive workplace culture. By providing coaching and mentoring, team-building activities, sensory-friendly social events, and clear communication, businesses can support neurodiverse employees and unlock their full potential in the workplace.

# Section 5 - Legal Considerations

## Overview of Legal Obligations

Businesses have a legal obligation to accommodate neurodiverse employees under the Americans with Disabilities Act (ADA) in the United States and the Equality Act 2010 in the United Kingdom. These laws require businesses to provide reasonable accommodations to employees with disabilities, including neurodiverse employees, to ensure that they can perform their jobs effectively.

Reasonable accommodations can include adjustments to work schedules, the provision of assistive technology or specialized equipment, or modifications to the physical work environment. Businesses are required to provide these accommodations unless doing so would result in an undue hardship, such as significant difficulty or expense.

Failure to comply with legal obligations to accommodate neurodiverse employees can result in legal consequences, including fines and lawsuits. It's important for businesses to understand their legal obligations and ensure compliance to avoid these consequences.

Additionally, businesses should recognize that accommodating neurodiverse employees is not only a legal obligation but also a moral imperative. Providing accommodations for neurodiverse employees can promote a more inclusive and diverse workplace culture that benefits all employees.

In conclusion, businesses have a legal obligation to accommodate neurodiverse employees under the ADA and Equality Act 2010. Failure to comply with these obligations can result in legal consequences, and it's important for businesses to understand their legal obligations and ensure compliance. However, accommodating neurodiverse employees is also a moral imperative that promotes a more inclusive and diverse workplace culture.

## Disclosure and Confidentiality

Neurodiverse employees may choose to disclose their condition to their employer in order to request accommodations or receive support in the workplace. It's important for businesses to create a culture that encourages disclosure and ensures confidentiality for neurodiverse employees.

Under the ADA and Equality Act 2010, employers are required to keep information about employees' disabilities confidential. This includes information about an employee's neurodivergent condition, medical documentation, and any accommodations that have been provided.

Disclosure can be a difficult decision for neurodiverse employees, as they may fear discrimination or negative consequences in the workplace. To create a supportive environment for disclosure, businesses should provide education and resources for employees and managers to better understand neurodiversity and accommodations.

Businesses should also create a clear process for requesting accommodations, including a designated point of contact for employees to request accommodations and a clear process for reviewing and responding to these requests.

In addition to providing a supportive environment for disclosure, businesses should also ensure that they are not discriminating against neurodiverse employees in the hiring process. This includes ensuring that job descriptions and interviews do not discriminate against candidates with neurodivergent conditions and providing accommodations during the application process if needed.

In conclusion, creating a culture of disclosure and confidentiality is essential for supporting neurodiverse employees and complying with legal obligations under the ADA and Equality Act 2010. By providing education and resources, creating a clear process for requesting accommodations, and ensuring non-discrimination in the hiring process, businesses can create an inclusive and supportive workplace culture for all employees.

# Case Law and Precedent

Legal cases and precedent have played a significant role in shaping the legal landscape around accommodations for neurodiverse employees. Here are a few examples:

- **In the US,** a 2015 case involving the grocery store chain Kroger set a precedent for the importance of providing accommodations for employees with autism. The case was settled for $150,000 and Kroger agreed to improve its training for managers and provide accommodations such as noise-cancelling headphones and a break area for employees with autism.
- **In the UK,** a 2016 case involving the retail giant John Lewis set a precedent for the legal obligation to accommodate employees with dyslexia. The employee in the case was awarded £65,000 after being dismissed for poor performance related to his dyslexia. The case highlighted the importance of providing accommodations such as specialized software and extra time for completing tasks.
- **In both the US and the UK,** legal cases have emphasized the importance of involving employees in the accommodation process and ensuring that accommodations are effective and meet their specific needs.

Businesses can learn from these cases and precedent to ensure compliance with legal obligations and provide effective accommodations for neurodiverse employees. It's important to involve neurodiverse employees in the accommodation process, provide clear communication and resources, and ensure that accommodations are effective and meeting the needs of employees.

In conclusion, legal cases and precedent have played a significant role in shaping the legal landscape around accommodations for neurodiverse employees. Businesses can learn from these cases and precedent to ensure compliance with legal obligations and provide effective accommodations for neurodiverse employees. It's important to involve neurodiverse employees in the accommodation process and ensure that accommodations are effective and meeting the needs of employees.

# Section 6 - Creating an Inclusive Workplace Culture

# Understanding Neurodiversity and Accommodations

Understanding neurodiversity and accommodations is essential for creating an inclusive workplace culture that values diversity and promotes success for all employees. Neurodiverse employees may have unique needs and strengths that require accommodations to ensure they can perform their jobs effectively.

To create an inclusive workplace culture, it's important to provide education and resources for managers and co-workers to better understand the needs of neurodiverse employees and how to provide effective accommodations. This can include providing training on neurodiversity, accommodations, and effective communication strategies.

It's also important to involve neurodiverse employees in the accommodation process to ensure that accommodations are effective and meet their specific needs. This can involve providing a designated point of contact for employees to request accommodations, regular check-ins to ensure that accommodations are meeting their needs, and creating a culture that encourages open communication about accommodations and challenges.

Additionally, businesses should ensure that they are not making assumptions about neurodiverse employees or stereotyping them based on their condition. It's important to recognize the unique strengths and abilities that neurodiverse employees bring to the workplace and create a culture that values diversity and promotes success for all employees.

In conclusion, understanding neurodiversity and accommodations is essential for creating an inclusive workplace culture that values diversity and promotes success for all employees. By providing education and resources, involving neurodiverse employees in the accommodation process, and creating a culture that values diversity and promotes success for all employees, businesses can create an inclusive workplace culture that benefits all employees.

## Building an Inclusive Culture

Building an inclusive workplace culture that values diversity and promotes success for all employees is essential for supporting neurodiverse employees and promoting a positive work environment. Here are some strategies for building an inclusive culture:

- **Employee Resource Groups (ERGs):** ERGs are groups of employees who share a common characteristic, such as a neurodivergent condition. ERGs can provide a supportive community for employees, promote awareness and understanding of neurodiversity, and provide feedback to the business on ways to improve the workplace for neurodiverse employees.
- **Mentorship Programs:** Mentorship programs can provide neurodiverse employees with guidance and support from experienced professionals within the business. Mentors can provide advice on navigating the workplace, developing skills, and advancing in their careers.
- **Training Programs:** Training programs for managers and employees can provide education and resources on neurodiversity and accommodations, as well as effective communication strategies and ways to recognize and address stigma and stereotypes.
- **Leadership Commitment:** Creating an inclusive workplace culture requires a commitment from the top. Leaders should communicate the importance of diversity and inclusion, set an example for managers and employees, and ensure that the business is providing effective accommodations and support for neurodiverse employees.

In conclusion, building an inclusive workplace culture that values diversity and promotes success for all employees is essential for supporting neurodiverse employees and promoting a positive work environment. Employee resource groups, mentorship programs, training programs, and leadership commitment are all strategies that can help build an inclusive culture. By creating an inclusive workplace culture that values diversity and promotes success for all employees, businesses can support the success of all employees, including neurodiverse employees.

## Supporting Career Development

Supporting the career development of neurodiverse employees is essential for creating an inclusive workplace culture that values diversity and promotes success for all employees. Here are some strategies for supporting career development:

- **Coaching and Mentoring:** Providing coaching and mentoring for neurodiverse employees can help them develop skills, navigate the workplace, and advance in their careers. Mentors and coaches can provide guidance on communication, problem-solving, and other skills that are essential for success in the workplace.
- **Employee Development Plans:** Employee development plans can help neurodiverse employees set goals, identify areas for improvement, and plan career advancement. Development plans can include training programs, coaching and mentoring, and other opportunities for growth and advancement.
- **Leadership Training:** Providing leadership training for neurodiverse employees can help them develop skills and competencies needed for leadership roles. This can include training on communication, team building, problem-solving, and other skills that are essential for effective leadership.

In conclusion, supporting the career development of neurodiverse employees is essential for creating an inclusive workplace culture that values diversity and promotes success for all employees. Coaching and mentoring, employee development plans, and leadership training are all strategies that can help support career development. By supporting the career development of neurodiverse employees, businesses can promote a positive work environment, foster employee engagement and retention, and unlock the full potential of their workforce.

# Addressing Stigma and Stereotypes

Addressing stigma and stereotypes is essential for creating an inclusive workplace culture that values diversity and promotes success for all employees. Stereotypes and stigmas can negatively impact the work environment, contribute to discrimination, and limit opportunities for neurodiverse employees. Here are some strategies for addressing stigma and stereotypes:

- **Language and Communication:** The language and communication used in the workplace can have a significant impact on the work environment for neurodiverse employees. Using inclusive language and avoiding derogatory terms or slang can help create a more positive work environment. Clear communication is also essential to ensure that neurodiverse employees understand expectations and can effectively perform their jobs.
- **Recognition of Strengths:** Neurodiverse employees have unique strengths and abilities that can be valuable in the workplace. Recognizing these strengths and providing opportunities for neurodiverse employees to use their strengths can help foster a more inclusive work environment.
- **Training and Education:** Providing training and education for managers and co-workers on neurodiversity and accommodations can help increase awareness and understanding of the needs of neurodiverse employees. This can include training on communication, problem-solving, and other skills that are essential for success in the workplace.
- **Involvement of Neurodiverse Employees:** Involving neurodiverse employees in decision-making processes and creating opportunities for their input can help ensure that accommodations and support meet their needs. This

can also help promote a more inclusive work environment by recognizing the value and expertise of neurodiverse employees.

In conclusion, addressing stigma and stereotypes is essential for creating an inclusive workplace culture that values diversity and promotes success for all employees. Strategies such as language and communication, recognition of strengths, training and education, and involvement of neurodiverse employees can help address stigma and promote a more positive work environment. By creating a more inclusive work environment, businesses can promote employee engagement and retention, unlock the full potential of their workforce, and create a more positive brand reputation.

# Section 7 - The Business Case for Neurodiversity

## Increased Innovation

Neurodiverse employees can bring unique perspectives and ways of thinking to the workplace that can lead to increased innovation and problem-solving. For example, individuals with autism may have a heightened attention to detail and exceptional memory skills, while individuals with ADHD may have high levels of creativity and an ability to generate ideas quickly. By accommodating these unique strengths and perspectives, businesses can unlock the full potential of their workforce and foster a culture of innovation.

There are many examples of neurodiverse individuals who have made significant contributions to the business world. For example, Temple Grandin, a professor of animal science who is on the autism spectrum, has revolutionized the livestock industry by designing more humane animal handling systems. Similarly, John Elder Robison, an author and entrepreneur who is on the autism spectrum, has founded several successful technology companies and is a recognized expert in the field of electronics.

In conclusion, by accommodating neurodiverse employees and recognizing their unique strengths and perspectives, businesses can foster a culture of innovation and problem-solving. This can lead to significant advancements and breakthroughs in the business world. By promoting diversity and inclusion in the workplace, businesses can unlock the full potential of their workforce and reap the benefits of a more innovative, productive, and engaged workforce.

## Improved Productivity

Providing effective accommodations and support for neurodiverse employees can lead to improved productivity and performance in the workplace. For example, individuals with dyslexia may benefit from assistive technology or extra time to complete written tasks, while individuals with ADHD may benefit from structured work environments and clear expectations.

There are many examples of businesses that have seen improvements in productivity and performance as a result of accommodating neurodiverse employees. For example, Microsoft has an autism hiring program and has found that neurodiverse employees are often highly productive and have a low turnover rate. Similarly, SAP, a software company, has found that providing accommodations for neurodiverse employees has resulted in improved productivity and employee retention.

By accommodating the needs of neurodiverse employees, businesses can unlock their full potential and improve their overall productivity and performance. By creating an inclusive work environment that values diversity and promotes success for all employees, businesses can improve employee engagement and retention, and promote a more positive work environment.

In conclusion, by accommodating neurodiverse employees and providing effective support and accommodations, businesses can improve their productivity and performance. This can lead to a more engaged and productive workforce, improved employee retention, and a more positive work environment overall.

## Employee Engagement and Retention

Creating an inclusive workplace culture that values diversity and promotes success for all employees can lead to increased employee engagement and retention, including for neurodiverse employees. By accommodating the needs of neurodiverse employees and creating a positive work environment, businesses can foster a sense of belonging and inclusion for all employees.

Neurodiverse employees may face challenges in the workplace related to communication, social interaction, and other areas. By providing effective support and accommodations, businesses can help these employees overcome these challenges and thrive in their roles. This can lead to increased employee engagement and retention, as neurodiverse employees feel valued and supported in their work.

There are many examples of businesses that have seen improvements in employee engagement and retention as a result of creating an inclusive workplace culture. For example, Ernst & Young has a neurodiversity program that provides support and accommodations for employees with neurodivergent conditions. As a result, the company has seen improved employee engagement and retention, as well as increased diversity in its workforce.

In conclusion, by creating an inclusive workplace culture that values diversity and promotes success for all employees, businesses can improve employee engagement and retention, including for neurodiverse employees. By providing effective support and accommodations, businesses can help neurodiverse employees overcome challenges and thrive in their roles, leading to a more engaged and productive workforce overall.

## Positive Brand Reputation

Creating an inclusive workplace culture that values diversity and promotes success for all employees can also lead to a more positive brand reputation for businesses. In today's increasingly socially conscious world, customers and stakeholders are increasingly drawn to companies that demonstrate a commitment to diversity and inclusion.

By promoting diversity and inclusion in the workplace and accommodating the needs of neurodiverse employees, businesses can improve their brand reputation and attract more customers and stakeholders. This can lead to increased brand loyalty and customer satisfaction.

There are many examples of businesses that have seen improvements in brand reputation as a result of promoting diversity and inclusion in the workplace. For example, the bank Santander has received recognition for its neurodiversity program, which provides support and accommodations for neurodiverse employees. This has helped the company to build a more positive brand reputation and attract customers who value diversity and inclusion.

In conclusion, by promoting diversity and inclusion in the workplace and accommodating the needs of neurodiverse employees, businesses can improve their brand reputation and attract more customers and stakeholders. This can lead to increased brand loyalty and customer satisfaction, and ultimately drive business success.

# Section 7 – Concluding Remarks and Resources

# Conclusion

In conclusion, this white paper has explored the topic of neurodiversity in the workplace, including what it is, why it's important, and how businesses can effectively accommodate the needs of neurodiverse employees. We have discussed the various neurodivergent conditions that can affect employees and the challenges they may face in the workplace. We have also explored the legal considerations and provided examples of businesses that have successfully accommodated neurodiverse employees and fostered an inclusive workplace culture.

Through our exploration, we have found that accommodating neurodiverse employees can lead to significant benefits for businesses, including increased innovation, productivity, employee engagement and retention, and a more positive brand reputation. By recognizing the unique strengths and abilities of neurodiverse employees and providing effective support and accommodations, businesses can unlock the full potential of their workforce and foster a culture of innovation and problem-solving.

It's important to recognize that promoting diversity and inclusion in the workplace is not only the right thing to do, but also makes good business sense. By creating an inclusive workplace culture that values diversity and promotes success for all employees, businesses can improve their overall productivity and performance, attract and retain top talent, and build a more positive brand reputation.

As we continue to navigate the challenges of the modern workplace, it's essential that businesses recognize the value of neurodiversity and work to accommodate the needs of all employees. By doing so, we can build a more inclusive and successful business world for everyone.

# Additional Resources

Here are a few UK resources related to neurodiversity in the workplace that readers may find helpful:

- **The National Autistic Society** - This UK-based charity offers a variety of resources for employers and employees related to autism in the workplace, including advice on accommodations and support. https://www.autism.org.uk
- **ACAS** - The Advisory, Conciliation and Arbitration Service offers free guidance on disability discrimination in the workplace. https://www.acas.org.uk/disability-at-work
- **The Dyslexia Association** - This UK-based charity offers resources and support for individuals with dyslexia and their employers, including advice on accommodations and training. https://www.bdadyslexia.org.uk
- **The ADHD Foundation** - This UK-based charity offers resources and support for individuals with ADHD and their employers, including advice on accommodations and training. https://www.adhdfoundation.org.uk
- **Business Disability Forum** - This UK-based organization offers resources and support for businesses related to disability and inclusion in the workplace, including information on accommodations for neurodiverse employees. https://businessdisabilityforum.org.uk

These resources can provide valuable information and support for employers and employees looking to promote neurodiversity and create a more inclusive workplace culture.

Here are a few US-based resources related to neurodiversity in the workplace that readers may find helpful:

- **The Job Accommodation Network (JAN)** - This US-based service provides free consulting services on accommodations for employees with disabilities, including neurodivergent conditions. https://askjan.org

- **The National Institute of Mental Health (NIMH)** - This US-based organization provides resources and information on mental health and related conditions, including neurodivergent conditions such as ADHD and autism. https://www.nimh.nih.gov
- **The American Association of People with Disabilities (AAPD)** - This US-based organization advocates for the rights of people with disabilities and provides resources for employers related to disability inclusion and accommodations. https://www.aapd.com
- **The Autism Society** - This US-based organization provides resources and support for individuals with autism and their families, as well as information for employers on accommodations and best practices. https://autismsociety.org
- **The Learning Disabilities Association of America (LDA)** - This US-based organization provides resources and support for individuals with learning disabilities and their families, as well as information for employers on accommodations and support. https://ldaamerica.org

These resources can provide valuable information and support for employers and employees looking to promote neurodiversity and create a more inclusive workplace culture in the US.

# Further Reading

We recommend these publications (links to Amazon):

**Neurodiversity in the Workplace: How to Create a Neurodiverse Inclusive Workplace**

https://amzn.to/3z4HMVd

**Neurodiversity in the Workplace: Interests, Issues, and Opportunities**

https://amzn.to/3LRxf7s

**Generation A: Research on Autism in the Workplace (Emerald Studies in Workplace Neurodiversity)**

https://amzn.to/40illHT

**The Pocket Guide to Neurodiversity**

https://amzn.to/3LTtnCU

**Untypical: How the World Isn't Built for Autistic People and What We Should All Do About It**

https://amzn.to/3LNA2hF

**Neurodiversity at Work: Drive Innovation, Performance and Productivity with a Neurodiverse Workforce**

https://amzn.to/42CTSIL

**The Neurodiverse Workplace: An Employer's Guide to Managing and Working with Neurodivergent Employees, Clients and Customers**

https://amzn.to/42DJQB1

# About HRreview.co.uk

This ebook is brought to you by the team at HRreview.

https://www.hrreview.co.uk/ is the UK's leading independent HR news, information, opinion and analysis resource dedicated to human resources and related professionals.

**Updated news items are posted daily** and there are regular updates to the features and analysis section, looking in depth at the latest HR issues and trends. We bring together some of the industry's key thought leaders and experienced practitioners to give you the best insight into the world of HR.

Our online magazine is supported by a series of **daily, weekly and monthly email newslette**rs that allow you to get the latest HR content that you want straight to your inbox. To choose the topics that suit you, please register here https://www.hrreview.co.uk/signup.

You can also be a part of our extensive **HRr professional communities** by following us on social media and joining us on **Linkedin** https://www.linkedin.com/groups/2061371/, where we post the best of our news and features throughout the week, both in our main group and our subgroups dedicated to discussion and networking on different topic areas. Follow us on **Facebook** https://www.facebook.com/HRreviewUK and on **Twitter** https://twitter.com/hrreview

Our series of **HR webinars**, https://www.hrreview.co.uk/free-webinars, gathers together leading experts for discussion and debate on the latest HR talking points, including assessing the impact of politics and elections on HR, interpreting new employment legislation and exploring case studies on HR practice with some of the UK's highest profile organisations. You can access these hour-long webinar sessions, entirely for free, by visiting the https://www.hrreview.co.uk/inside-hr-webinars/our-webinars/55137.

Our **podcast**, https://www.hrreview.co.uk/podcast, can be downloaded from all podcast apps and you can also listen on our website https://www.hrreview.co.uk/hr-in-review-podcast-episodes.